Praying Leviticus

The Living Word Series

Praying through the Bible, one book at a time.

Praying Leviticus

Prayers for Holiness, Worship, and the Sacred Ordinary

GRAHAM JOSEPH HILL

Eagna Publishing • Sydney, Australia

PRAYING LEVITICUS
Prayers for Holiness, Worship, and the Sacred Ordinary

Published by: Eagna Publishing (Sydney, Australia)
eagnapublishing@icloud.com
Cover and interior design: Graham Joseph Hill
www.grahamjosephhill.com

paperback isbn: 978-1-7644455-3-5
ebook isbn: 978-1-7644455-4-2
version number: 2025-01-01

NATIONAL LIBRARY OF AUSTRALIA

A catalogue record for this book is available from the National Library of Australia

Contents

Prologue: When Holiness Draws Near

Before sacrifice had shape or structure,
before altars gleamed with oil and light,
there was only a people stunned by nearness,
a God who refused to stay at a distance,
a Presence that filled the tent
like breath fills a fragile lung.

They didn't yet know how to live with such glory.
How to carry fire without being consumed,
how to bear the weight of mercy,
how to walk in a world where heaven pitched its tent on earth.
So, God taught them slowly,
through offerings and anointing,
through feasts and boundaries,
through rhythms of rest and remembrance.

Holiness was never a cage.
It was an invitation.
A way of life shaped by the One
who binds justice to compassion
and purity to neighbor-love.
A way for wounded wanderers
to become a kingdom of priests,
bearing light, tending fire,
living lives fragrant with devotion.

And still the Spirit moves through the pages of Leviticus,
through the smoke of surrender,
through the blood that heals what sin has broken,
through the beauty of consecrated work,
through the silence of Sabbath
where the world is allowed to breathe again.

The same voice that called Israel into holiness
speaks to us even now:
"Be mine. Be like me. Be whole."

Each prayer in Leviticus is an approach and an offering,
a letting go and a drawing near,
a practice of becoming people
who can carry the Presence
without fear, without pretense,
with hearts set on the fire that sets all things right.

In praying Leviticus,
we remember that holiness is a pathway,
a deep belonging,
a personal and communal way of being,
and a life continually turned
toward the God who dwells among us.

Introduction: Praying the Presence

Leviticus is the story of nearness: the God who chooses to dwell among a wandering people, and the people learning (slowly, reverently) how to live with that holy fire in their midst.

If Exodus reveals a God who delivers, Leviticus reveals a God who stays. It begins with a Voice calling from the tent of meeting. It unfolds into a vision of life ordered around divine presence: sacrifice and Sabbath, purity and justice, priests and people, all woven into a single fabric of communion. Leviticus is the grammar of holiness. To pray Leviticus is to step into the rhythms that make belonging possible: the holy insistence that God isn't distant, and therefore life must be reshaped from the inside out.

Praying through Leviticus awakens us to the God who sanctifies not only rituals but hearts. We begin at the altar, naming what needs surrender (fear, guilt, resentment, greed), and we follow the long, tender path toward wholeness. Through offerings and ordinations, feasts and fasts, boundaries and blessings, we learn that holiness isn't mere rule-keeping but relationship: God drawing us near, God forming our character, God teaching us to bear divine presence with integrity and joy.

These prayers invite encounter, not dissection. They turn laws into liturgy, sacrifice into surrender, and instruction into intimacy. In praying Leviticus, we discover that our own stories breathe within its structure: our longing for forgiveness in the burnt offerings, our hunger for justice in the holiness code, our weariness seeking rest in Sabbath rhythms, our fractured lives yearning for the healing atonement brings.

This book is for those longing for nearness, for cleansing, for a life shaped by divine presence. Pray it slowly (alone or together), letting its rhythms remake your own. Let each chapter become a doorway into deeper communion, into a holiness that liberates rather than constricts, into the mystery of a God who dares to dwell with humanity.

Leviticus is God's invitation still extended: a journey from distance to delight, from chaos to consecration, from ordinary life to a life infused with the beauty of God's presence.

The Living Word Series: A Guide to the Prayer Pattern

Each prayer in this series follows an eight-movement rhythm shaped by Scripture's own way of speaking with God.

This pattern is a pathway (flexible, honest, spacious) allowing every chapter of the Bible to breathe its truth into our lives.

I invite you to walk this rhythm slowly, letting each movement form your heart as you pray.

1. *Invocation: Naming God as the Text Reveals God*

Every chapter unveils a facet of God's character.

We begin by addressing God with the images, names, and actions drawn directly from the passage.

Here, prayer begins in wonder.

2. *Confession: Naming Our Distortion of That Revelation*

Standing before the God revealed, we acknowledge the ways we fall short: personally, communally, and systemically.

This movement is truth-telling, not shame.

3. *Lament: Naming the Wounds of the World*

Every text encounters a wound in creation or in us.

Here we let the chapter's sorrow speak alongside today's sufferings, refusing denial or indifference.

4. *Hope in God: Turning Toward Divine Faithfulness*

This is the hinge of the prayer.

We recall who God is, what God has done, and how God remains present in our lives.

Hope isn't optimism but trust.

5. Petition: Asking Boldly for Transformation

Rooted in the text's longings, we ask God to act.

We petition for justice, mercy, courage, healing: whatever the passage calls us to desire.

6. Commitment: Offering Ourselves to God's Work

Grace invites participation.

Here we pledge to walk in the light we've seen, to embody what we've prayed.

7. Eschatological Hope: Lifting Our Eyes to God's Future

Every chapter leans toward the fullness of God's kingdom.

We remember the promised renewal that holds all our prayers in hope.

8. Doxology / Assurance: Ending in Praise and Trust

The prayer concludes in praise: naming the goodness and nearness of the Triune God.

We rest in the assurance that God is faithful, now and forever.

This prayer structure mirrors the movement of the Psalms and the spiritual life itself: from naming, to truth-telling, to sorrow, to hope, to praise. The pattern holds lament and joy together so that neither becomes shallow: the honesty of pain leading us into the freedom of worship.

May this rhythm guide you as you pray your way through Scripture: honestly, courageously, and with the deep trust that the Living Word still speaks, still heals, still leads us home.

As you journey through these prayers, pause often. Let specific lines become your own. Insert the names of your community, your city, your wounds. Use silence as part of the conversation. These prayers aren't substitutes for Scripture, but doorways into it: a way to hear the ancient stories breathe again in our century.

Leviticus begins in invitation and ends in communion. It assures us that the God who drew near to a fragile people still desires nearness, still teaches hearts how to live with fire in their midst, still transforms ordinary lives into places of encounter. The story moves from offering to intimacy, from cleansing to consecration, from scattered rhythms to a life woven around divine presence. May these prayers teach us to see the world as Leviticus sees it: charged with holiness, sustained by mercy, shaped by rhythms of rest and justice, and held by the God who invites every wandering heart into wholeness, belonging, and radiant love.

An Offering of the Whole Heart (Leviticus 1)

God who invites us to draw near,
    you call your people to bring what's costly,
    to come without pretense,
    to offer not scraps but the fullness of our devotion.
You meet us at the altar with fire that purifies,
    not consumes.

We confess how often our offerings are partial.
We hold back the best parts of ourselves,
    we give you leftovers rather than love,
    we approach your presence with distracted hearts,
    hoping for transformation without surrender.
We fear the vulnerability of being fully known,
    and avoid your holiness and power.

We lament the parts of our lives still untouched by your flame,
    desires we refuse to yield,
    habits that cling like old garments,
    wounds we hide rather than place upon your altar.
We grieve the harm caused by half-hearted faith,
    and the ways our divided devotion dulls our witness.

Yet you, O Lord, receive us with patient mercy.
You call for offerings not to burden us
    but to free us from false gods.
You meet us in the smoke that rises,

in the fire that refines,
in the surrender that becomes communion,
in the willingness to give ourselves completely,
to your righteousness, justice, holiness, and love.
Even now, you welcome us into a deeper nearness,
not through perfection, but through willingness.

So, teach us to offer our whole selves.
Let our prayers be wholehearted,
let our repentance be honest,
let our worship be unreserved.
Burn away what keeps us distant,
and kindle in us a devotion that doesn't waver.
Even now, place upon the altar
what we can't heal or carry alone.

Make us a people who come before you with open hands,
who give with joy,
surrender with trust,
and rise from the altar transformed by love.

Until every life becomes a living offering,
until fear yields to faith,
until holiness becomes our home,
keep drawing us near by your refining fire.

Blessed are you, God who receives our offering.
Blessed are you, Christ who gives himself wholly for us.
Blessed are you, Spirit who makes our lives aflame with love.

Amen.

A Gift of Daily Bread (Leviticus 2)

God who receives the work of human hands,
>you welcome offerings made not of spectacle but substance,
>grain gathered from fields,
>flour crushed and sifted,
>oil poured with care,
>frankincense rising like gratitude made fragrant.

You teach us that holiness is woven into the everyday.

We confess how quickly gratitude slips from our hearts.
We take harvest for granted,
>treat nourishment as ordinary,
>forget that every grain is grace.

We withhold thanksgiving
>even as we cling to abundance,
>and we fail to honor you
>with the work shaped by our own hands.

We lament the places where daily bread is scarce,
>families unsure of tomorrow's meals,
>laborers exploited for the world's consumption,
>lands depleted by greed,
>communities fractured by inequity and hunger.

We grieve every table where abundance sits beside emptiness,
>and every life that knows more toil than joy.

Yet you, O Lord, welcome simple offerings with joy.
You sanctify gifts that rise from gratitude,
>   you bless the ordinary with divine nearness,
>   you turn daily work into worship.
You teach us that salt sustains covenant,
>   that oil softens what's brittle,
>   that bread offered freely becomes communion.
Even now, you receive our humble gifts,
>   the work of our days,
>   the fruit of our labor,
>   our whispered thanks carried on unseen incense.

So, shape our hearts for gratitude.
Teach us to offer what's honest,
>   to honor you in our rhythms of work,
>   to bless others with the abundance we've been given.
Let generosity flavor our living,
>   and justice season our communities.
Even now, make our daily bread holy,
>   and our daily work a fragrant offering.

Make us a people who offer ourselves with joy,
>   simple, steady, wholehearted,
>   bearing gratitude as our truest gift.

Until every table is full,
>   until every field is blessed,
>   until your kingdom feeds the world with peace,
>   keep receiving the work we place before you.

Blessed are you, God of grain and grace.

Blessed are you, Christ our bread of life.

Blessed are you, Spirit who fills our offerings with fragrance.

Amen.

The Table of Peace (Leviticus 3)

God who welcomes us into shared fellowship,
      you invite your people to offer not out of fear
      but out of gratitude and joy.
You prepare a table where peace is tasted,
      where offering becomes communion,
      and where your presence gathers us into wholeness.

We confess how often we resist your peace.
We cling to grudges like shields,
      avoid the cost of reconciliation,
      prefer distance over vulnerability.
We come to your table with divided hearts,
      forgetting that peace with you
      calls us into peace with one another.

We lament the fractures that scar our communities,
      families estranged,
      neighbors at odds,
      nations in turmoil,
      churches torn by rivalry or fear,
      people avoiding the repentance that leads to peace with you.
We grieve the violence, subtle or seen,
      that makes fellowship fragile
      and communion rare.

Yet you, O Lord, delight in peace that's shared.

You receive offerings meant to heal,
>> you invite your people to eat in your presence,
>> you sanctify fellowship as holy ground.
The fat consumed upon the altar
>> becomes a sign of life restored,
>> relationships mended,
>> trust renewed.
Even now, you call us back to your table,
>> to sit, to reconcile,
>> to feast in the light of your gentle presence.

So, make us artisans of peace.
Teach us to release what poisons our fellowship,
>> to seek forgiveness boldly,
>> to welcome those we once kept at arm's length,
>> to live in peace with you because of Jesus Christ.
Let our meals become liturgies of grace,
>> our homes places of welcome,
>> our lives offerings of reconciliation.
Even now, prepare a feast within us
>> that nourishes others with your peace.

Make us a people who live from your table,
>> sharing generously,
>> forgiving readily,
>> loving deeply,
>> walking gently,
>> following Christ, the divine peace offering.

Until every conflict yields to compassion,
>> until enmity is erased by communion,
>> until your kingdom becomes a feast without fear,
>> keep us gathered in your peace.

Blessed are you, God of fellowship.
Blessed are you, Christ our peace offering.
Blessed are you, Spirit who knits hearts together.

Amen.

For the Sins We Didn't See (Leviticus 4)

God who reveals what we overlook,
>you shine light into the secret corners of our hearts,
>you uncover harm we never intended,
>you teach us that sin isn't only rebellion
>but the ripple of our unawareness.

You make a path back to wholeness
>before we even know we need one.

We confess the unintended wrongs we carry.
Words spoken without care,
>choices made without wisdom,
>habits formed without attention,
>all of them leaving marks we never saw.

We confess the harm done in ignorance,
>the wounds caused by haste or indifference,
>the failures we barely recognized.

We lament the unseen fractures around us,
>relationships strained by thoughtless actions,
>communities weakened by small but steady neglect,
>systems bent by choices no one meant to harm.

We grieve the suffering
>born from what was overlooked rather than desired.

Yet you, O Lord, are merciful in your clarity.
You provide offerings for the unaware,

cleansing for the unintentional,
    restoration for the wounds we discover too late.
Your forgiveness doesn't wait for perfection,
        it invites honesty,
        it restores dignity,
        it binds the community back together.
Even now, you gently reveal what needs healing,
        and offer grace for every unmeant wound.

So, teach us to walk with greater attentiveness.
Sharpen our compassion,
        slow our reactions,
        soften our assumptions.
Give us courage to confess what we missed,
        and humility to seek repair.
Let your Spirit train our instincts toward love,
        that our lives may cause less harm
        and offer more healing.
Even now, cleanse what we didn't see
        and renew what we didn't guard.

Make us a people who repair the world,
        quick to acknowledge,
        quick to forgive,
        quick to repent,
        quick to embrace,
        quick to hope,
        quick to restore,
        quick to reconcile.

Until every hidden wound is healed,
until unintended harm is met with abundant grace,
until holiness restores what sin has frayed,

keep leading us toward truth.

Blessed are you, God who notices.
Blessed are you, Christ who restores.
Blessed are you, Spirit who convicts and comforts.

Amen.

The Courage to Make Things Right (Leviticus 5)

God who listens to honest hearts,
> you welcome confession not with punishment
> but with mercy that restores.
You teach us that truth-telling is sacred,
> that repair is holy work,
> and that forgiveness isn't an escape from responsibility
> but a pathway into peace and divine love.

We confess what we've failed to say and do.
The truth we withheld,
> the silence that harmed,
> the promises broken by neglect,
> the offerings withheld through fear or forgetfulness.
We confess the moments we turned from need,
> or looked away when honesty cost too much.

We lament the fractures left behind.
Relationships thinned by avoidance,
> trust weakened by half-truths,
> communities unsettled by harm unacknowledged.
We grieve the wounds that linger
> when courage falters
> and restitution seems impossible.

Yet you, O Lord, meet us in our failure with grace.
You provide offerings for confession,

pathways for restitution,
promises for those who come clean.
You show that forgiveness is never abstract:
it reaches toward the one harmed,
repairs what was damaged,
and restores dignity to all involved.
Even now, you invite us into truth that heals,
into responsibility that frees,
into mercy that makes us whole.

So, teach us the slow, brave work of repair.
Give us humility to admit fault,
wisdom to name harm,
eyes to see where we've wronged others,
hearts open to revelations of our sin,
courage to seek reconciliation,
desire to make and receive atonement,
and generosity to restore what we took or broke.
Let confession become liberation,
and restitution become worship.
Even now, awaken in us a tenderness
that refuses to leave wounds unattended.

Make us a people who mend what's torn,
quick to apologize,
quick to restore,
quick to offer grace.

Until every wrong is met with repair,
until every confession becomes a step toward wholeness,
until your mercy heals what truth reveals,
until we receive your abundant forgiveness,
until your grace, holiness, and love purifies us,

keep shaping us in your compassion,
keep fixing our eyes of Jesus Christ.

Blessed are you, God of restoration.
Blessed are you, Christ our atonement and peace.
Blessed are you, Spirit who empowers repair.

Amen.

Keeping the Fire Burning (Leviticus 6)

God who tends the altar through every ordinary day,
    you're present in the repeated and unseen,
    you dwell in the faithfulness that rises morning and evening,
    you entrust us with fire that must be guarded with care.

We confess how easily our devotion becomes intermittent.
We burn brightly for a moment, then grow distracted.
We neglect the slow disciplines that sustain love,
    delay restitution when it costs us,
    and forget that holiness is practiced daily,
    not proven occasionally.

We lament the damage caused by careless worship,
    fires left unattended,
    trust eroded by negligence,
    communities harmed when responsibility is ignored.
We grieve the quiet exhaustion of those who serve faithfully
    without recognition,
    and the wounds left when repair is postponed.

Yet you, O Lord, call us back to steady obedience.
You command the fire to keep burning,
    not for spectacle but for constancy.
You teach priests to tend embers before dawn,
    to remove yesterday's ashes,
    to make room for today's offering.

You bind forgiveness to repair
and worship to integrity.
Even now, you rekindle what's grown dim,
teaching us that faithfulness itself is holy fire.

So, train us in the grace of daily devotion.
Give us courage to make restitution without delay,
patience to tend small acts of faith,
and humility to return again and again to the altar.
Teach us to clear the ashes of old failures
and offer ourselves anew.
Even now, guard the flame within us,
steady, resilient, quietly radiant.

Make us a people who keep the fire burning,
honest in repair,
faithful in service,
attentive in prayer,
rooted in love.

Until every act becomes worship,
until faithfulness shapes our lives,
until your fire lights the whole earth,
keep us tending what you've entrusted to us.

Blessed are you, God of enduring flame.
Blessed are you, Christ our faithful offering.
Blessed are you, Spirit who keeps the fire alive.

Amen.

Remembering What's Given (Leviticus 7)

God who teaches us how to receive as well as give,
>   you gather your people around offerings shared,
>   meals remembered,
>   and gifts handled with reverence.
You remind us that holiness isn't only about approach,
>   but about how we carry what has been entrusted to us.

We confess how casually we treat sacred gifts.
We forget the cost behind generosity,
>   consume without gratitude,
>   and blur boundaries meant to protect life and love.
We take what's holy and make it ordinary,
>   what's communal and make it private,
>   what's shared and make it ours alone.

We lament the harm caused when reverence fades,
>   communities fractured by entitlement,
>   leaders who consume more than they serve,
>   tables where some feast while others go hungry.
We grieve how quickly gratitude erodes
>   when memory is short
>   and restraint feels burdensome.

Yet you, O Lord, order life with wisdom and care.
You teach your people to remember thanksgiving offerings,
>   to share peace meals in joy,

to honor what's set apart,
  to respect limits that guard the body and the community.
Your law forms a people capable of trust,
  capable of gratitude,
  capable of living together without harm.
Even now, you invite us to receive your gifts with care,
  to eat with awareness,
  to share with joy,
  to remember whose goodness sustains us.

So school us in grateful restraint.
Teach us to honor what's given,
  to share without hoarding,
  to remember the source of every good gift.
Let gratitude guide our consumption,
  and reverence shape our freedom.
Even now, train our desires
  so that abundance becomes blessing rather than burden.

You teach us that what's offered is never only personal.
Portions are shared,
  responsibilities distributed,
  holiness carried together.
You guard against secret consumption,
  against taking what was meant for the whole,
  against leaders feeding themselves while others watch hungrily.
You remind us that sacred gifts bind a community,
  that trust is built when what's holy
  is handled in the light.

Make us a people who remember,
>who give thanks before we take,
>who share before we store,
>who honor before we enjoy.

Until every table is shaped by gratitude,
>until every gift is handled with care,
>until your holiness blesses our common life,
>keep forming us in wisdom.

Blessed are you, God of every good gift.
Blessed are you, Christ who hosts us at the table of peace.
Blessed are you, Spirit who teaches us grateful living.

Amen.

Set Apart in the Sight of All (Leviticus 8)

God who forms servants in the open light,
     you call a whole community to witness consecration,
     you shape leaders not in secret ambition
     but in public obedience,
     washing, clothing, anointing,
     teaching us that holiness is learned before it's exercised.

We confess our impatience with formation.
We want authority without preparation,
     platform without process,
     calling without submission.
We resist being shaped by hands not our own
     and forget that service begins with surrender.

We lament the harm done when leaders are rushed or unformed,
     communities bruised by immaturity,
     trust broken by ego,
     holy spaces damaged by those
     not yet ready to carry their weight.
We grieve the cost paid
     when formation is skipped
     and humility dismissed as weakness.

Yet you, O Lord, consecrate with wisdom and care.
You gather the people to see what you're doing,
     you clothe your servants in garments not of self-importance

but of responsibility,
>   you anoint them with oil that marks belonging,
>   and blood that binds service to sacrifice.
Holiness isn't seized;
>   it's received.
Even now, you're forming leaders among us,
>   patiently, publicly,
>   with mercy that trains and love that steadies.

So teach us to submit to your forming work.
Wash us where pride clings,
>   clothe us where insecurity shows,
>   anoint us not for status but for service.
Give us courage to be shaped in community
>   and faith to trust the slow work of becoming.
Even now, set us apart with humility,
>   that our lives may bless rather than burden others.

Make us a people who honor formation,
>   who prepare before we presume,
>   who serve before we speak,
>   who carry authority lightly and love deeply.

Until every leader is shaped by faithfulness,
>   until service is rooted in reverence,
>   until holiness becomes visible as humility,
>   keep forming us in your presence.

Blessed are you, God who consecrates with care.
Blessed are you, Christ our servant and high priest.
Blessed are you, Spirit who forms us for holy work.

Amen.

When Glory Appears (Leviticus 9)

God who meets us when obedience takes its first steps,
      you receive offerings shaped by trembling hands,
      you bless a people learning how to serve,
      and you reveal your glory not in spectacle alone
      but in faithfulness offered before you.

We confess our fear of beginning.
We hesitate at the threshold of responsibility,
      afraid our service will fall short,
      afraid our obedience will be exposed.
We long for assurance before we act,
      forgetting that trust is often learned by doing.

We lament how easily confidence eclipses reverence,
      how quickly holy acts become routine,
      how service slips into performance,
      how blessing is sought without surrender.
We grieve communities hungry for God's presence
      but unwilling to approach with humility and care.

Yet you, O Lord, honor faithful obedience.
You receive the offerings of newly consecrated hands,
      you accept sacrifice brought with care and reverence,
      and you answer with fire that falls from heaven.
Your glory appears not to overwhelm
      but to affirm:

to bless what has been offered in trust.
Even now, you meet us at the altar of first obedience,
      confirming our service with your nearness,
      and reminding us that you're pleased to dwell among us.

So steady us as we serve, God of holy appearing.
Teach us to act without presumption,
      to obey without fear,
      to bless others before seeking our own reward.
Let our service rise from gratitude,
      and our leadership rest in reverence.
Even now, receive what we offer,
      small, sincere, and imperfect,
      and let your glory be known among us.

Make us a people who serve with awe,
      obedient before confident,
      faithful before successful,
      attentive before assured.

Until your glory fills every gathering,
      until your presence rests upon all our work,
      until heaven and earth rejoice together,
      keep us serving in your holy light.

Blessed are you, God who reveals your glory.
Blessed are you, Christ our perfect offering.
Blessed are you, Spirit who confirms our obedience with fire.

Amen.

When the Fire Consumes (Leviticus 10)

God of holy fire and awesome mystery,
>you're the One who can't be trifled with,
>the Presence who demands reverence,
>the Glory that won't be mocked.

You proved yourself holy among those who drew near,
>and you were honored in the sight of all the people.

Even when we don't understand your ways,
>you remain God.

We confess our presumption before you.

We approach your presence with careless hearts,
>offering unauthorized worship shaped by our preferences,
>bringing strange fire kindled by ambition or impatience
>rather than the flame you yourself have given.

We treat your commands as suggestions,
>your holiness as negotiable,
>your glory as something we can manage.

We lament the weight of this story:
>sons lost in a single moment,
>a father's silence heavier than words,
>grief forbidden its fullest expression,
>bodies carried out by cousins
>>while the anointing oil still glistened.

We grieve the cost of presumption in every age:
>leaders who mishandle sacred trust,

communities damaged by those who serve themselves
rather than the God they claim to represent.
We mourn all who've been burned by unholy fire
offered in your name.

Yet you, O Lord, aren't only consuming fire;
you're also patient mercy.
You continued with Aaron,
gave instruction rather than only judgment,
taught distinction between the holy and the common,
the clean and the unclean.
You didn't abandon your people in their grief;
you showed them how to move forward.
Even now, your holiness invites us to deeper reverence,
not to drive us away but to draw us closer
with proper awe.

So teach us, Holy One, to approach with trembling and trust.
Purify our worship of all that's unauthorized,
every innovation born of ego,
every shortcut that bypasses your way.
Give us discernment to know the difference
between holy fire and strange fire,
between what you've commanded
and what we've invented.
Even now, guard those who serve in sacred spaces
from pride that corrupts and haste that destroys.

Make us a people who honor your holiness,
who carry out our calling with sobriety and clarity,
who refuse to let familiarity breed contempt.
Help us distinguish between the sacred and the ordinary,
and teach those who come after us to do the same.

May our silence, like Aaron's,
    sometimes be the truest surrender
    when we can't understand your ways.

Until every act of worship is pure,
    until every leader serves with holy fear,
    until your glory fills the earth
    and none approach you carelessly,
    keep us walking in reverent faith.

Blessed are you, God who's holy beyond our reckoning.
Blessed are you, Christ who opened the way through your own sacrifice.
Blessed are you, Spirit who teaches us to worship in spirit and truth.

Amen.

Holiness at Every Table (Leviticus 11)

God who shapes your people through the ordinary,
 you teach holiness not only in the sanctuary
 but at every table, in every kitchen,
 in the daily rhythm of what we take into our bodies.
You brought your people out of Egypt
 to be yours,
 and you called them to live distinctly,
 set apart even in the choices they made each day.
You're holy,
 and you invite us into that holiness
 through the simplest acts of living.

We confess how carelessly we consume.
We fill ourselves without thought,
 swallowing what numbs rather than nourishes,
 feeding on fear, on gossip, on images that corrupt.
We forget that what we take in shapes what we become.
We resist the idea that holiness reaches into the everyday,
 preferring a faith that leaves our habits untouched.
We blur the lines between clean and unclean,
 sacred and profane,
 and wonder why our lives lack wholeness.

We lament the brokenness that touches our daily bread:
 food systems built on exploitation,
 creation groaning under greed,

bodies harmed by what was meant to sustain them.
We grieve the ways we've consumed without conscience,
    taken without thanksgiving,
    eaten the fruit of injustice without tasting its bitterness.
We mourn a world where some tables overflow
    while others sit empty,
    and discernment has been traded for appetite.

Yet you, O Lord, don't abandon us to our confusion.
You gave your people a way to remember
    with every bite, every meal, every choice:
    that they belong to you,
    that holiness is woven into flesh and bone,
    that even eating can be an act of worship.
You teach us to distinguish,
    to pay attention,
    to let the boundaries you set become pathways to freedom.
Even now, you call us to be holy as you're holy,
    whole and set apart,
    reflecting your character in our daily lives.

So give us discernment, God of wisdom.
Teach us to choose what gives life
    and refuse what brings death.
Help us see how the ordinary becomes sacred
    when offered to you with intention.
Guard what we take into our minds and hearts,
    our eyes and ears,
    our bodies and spirits.
Even now, make us attentive to the ways
    our choices shape our souls.

Make us a people of holy distinction,
        not in self-righteous separation,
        but in thoughtful consecration.
Let our tables become altars of gratitude,
        our kitchens places of prayer,
        our daily bread a reminder of your faithfulness.
Help us carry the discipline of discernment
        into all we consume:
        words, images, ideas, and desires.

Until every meal is shared in justice,
        until creation is restored to wholeness,
        until all that defiles is swallowed up
        in the holiness of your kingdom,
        keep forming us in the way of your set-apart people.

Blessed are you, God who makes us whole.
Blessed are you, Christ who feeds us with your own life.
Blessed are you, Spirit who sanctifies the ordinary.

Amen.

The Holiness of New Life (Leviticus 12)

God of life and new beginning,
>you hold the mystery of birth in your hands,
>the blood and labor,
>the cry and the breath,
>the exhaustion and the wonder.

You meet mothers in the rawness of their bodies,
>and you give them time:
>time to heal, time to bond,
>time to return to the rhythms of your presence.

You honor the sacred work of bringing life into the world
>with rituals of rest and restoration.

We confess how poorly we honor the vulnerable.
We rush mothers back to productivity,
>measure worth by output,
>and leave those who've labored to bring life
>to recover alone, unsupported, unseen.

We've treated bodies as inconveniences
>rather than temples of your creative power.

We've forgotten that transitions need tending,
>that thresholds are holy ground,
>that the work of nurturing life deserves honor and rest.

We lament the mothers who labor without support,
>who can't afford to rest,
>who carry children in bodies worn thin by poverty or violence.

We grieve the lives lost in childbirth,
  the babies who never drew breath,
  the grief that follows what should have been joy.
We mourn for those who long for children
  but find only empty arms,
  and for those whose bodies bear scars
  the world refuses to see.

Yet you, O Lord, see what's hidden.
You watched your own Son
  carried by a young woman
  who brought him to the temple
  with the offering of the poor:
  two turtledoves, two pigeons,
  the sign that you welcome all who come.
You provide for those who can't afford a lamb,
  because your grace meets us where we're.
Even now, you sanctify the seasons of our bodies
  and lead us gently back to wholeness.

So teach us, Lord, to honor life's thresholds.
Give rest to those who've given everything
  to bring new life into the world.
Surround the vulnerable with care,
  the exhausted with community,
  the grieving with tenderness.
Even now, bless those recovering
  from the holy labor of birth,
  and restore what's been depleted.

Make us a people who guard the sacred transitions,
  who make space for healing,
  who refuse to rush the weary back to work

before their bodies and souls are ready.
Help us build communities where mothers are honored,
    children are welcomed as blessing,
    and every body is treated as holy.

Until every birth is attended with dignity,
    until every mother finds rest and welcome,
    until the pain of labor gives way
    to the joy of your kingdom come,
    keep us tending the thresholds of life.

Blessed are you, God who knits life in the womb.
Blessed are you, Christ born of woman, offered in the temple.
Blessed are you, Spirit who renews and restores.

Amen.

Seen in Our Affliction (Leviticus 13)

God who sees what festers beneath the surface,
    you don't look away from the afflicted.
You instruct your priests to examine carefully,
    to look closely at the swelling,
        the rash, the raw and broken places,
    to wait, to watch, to distinguish
    between what heals and what spreads.
You give attention to the skin that shows
    what the heart can't hide,
    and you make room for time,
    for patient discernment,
    for bodies to be known before they're named.

We confess our fear of what's broken in us.
We hide our wounds rather than bring them to the light.
We cover what festers,
    ignore what spreads,
    and avoid the careful examination that leads to healing.
We've also been quick to pronounce others unclean,
    to cast out without patience,
    to isolate without love,
    to name disease when we should have waited and watched.

We lament the cry of the afflicted:
    those forced to tear their clothes,
    cover their faces,

and call out their own uncleanness.
We grieve the lonely ones,

    sent outside the camp,

    cut off from community,

    marked by sickness they didn't choose.
We mourn for all who live with afflictions

    that make them feel untouchable,

        unseen,

    beyond the reach of belonging.

Yet you, O Lord, don't abandon the afflicted.
Your examination isn't condemnation

    but the first step toward restoration.
You wait seven days, then seven more,

    giving time for what seemed unclean

    to fade and be pronounced whole.
And when your Son walked among us,

    he reached out his hand to touch the untouchable,

    saying, "I'm willing. Be clean."
Even now, you draw near to those the world pushes away.

So give us courage to be seen, O God.
Help us bring our hidden wounds into the light,

    trusting that examination leads to healing,

        not shame.
Give your people wisdom to discern

    what needs time, what needs care,

    what can heal if we're patient.
Even now, touch those who've been cast out,

    and speak the word that makes them clean.

Make us a people who examine with compassion,

    who wait before we pronounce,

who seek restoration rather than exclusion.
Teach us to be communities
    where the afflicted aren't abandoned
    but accompanied,
    where isolation, when needed, is surrounded by hope,
    and where the path back to belonging is always held open.

Until every wound is healed,
    until every exile returns to community,
    until no one cries "unclean" in despair,
    keep us reaching toward those who suffer.

Blessed are you, God who examines with mercy.
Blessed are you, Christ who touches the untouchable.
Blessed are you, Spirit who restores what was cast out.

Amen.

The Long Way Home (Leviticus 14)

God who makes a way back,
      you don't leave the healed outside the camp.
You send the priest to meet them where they're,
      beyond the boundaries of belonging,
      and you design rituals rich with meaning:
      two birds, one slain and one released,
      cedar and hyssop and scarlet yarn,
      blood sprinkled seven times,
      oil applied to ear and thumb and toe.
You restore the whole person,
      body and soul,
      and you bring the outcast home.

We confess how often we forget to welcome back
      those who've walked through affliction.
We're quicker to exclude than to restore,
      quicker to judge than to journey alongside.
We grow impatient with the slow rituals of healing,
      the seven days and then the eighth,
      the careful steps that mark the path
      from isolation to community.
We've left people stranded
      between their healing and their homecoming.

We lament all who've been healed
      but never fully welcomed back.

We grieve those who still live outside the camp
      in shame and stigma,
      long after their bodies have recovered.
We mourn the poor who can't afford
      the offerings that mark their restoration,
      whose path home is blocked
      by what they don't have.
We weep for every person
      whose healing brought no celebration.

Yet you, O Lord, go out to meet the healed.
You make provision for those experiencing poverty:
      two doves instead of lambs,
      grace for those who've nothing but their need.
You anoint ear, hand, and foot
      with blood and oil,
      reclaiming every part for holy purpose:
      what we hear, what we do, where we walk.
You release the living bird into open fields,
      a sign that affliction has flown,
      that freedom has come.
Even now, you lead the exiled home.

So come to us outside our camps, O God.
Meet us in the places of our exile
      and begin the slow, sure work of restoration.
Pronounce clean what's been healed.
Anoint us for new life:
      ears to hear your voice again,
      hands to do your work,
      feet to walk in your ways.
Even now, release what has bound us
      and bring us back to belonging.

Make us a people who practice restoration,
    who go outside the camp to find the healed,
    who create rituals of welcome
    for those who've walked through suffering.
Teach us patience with the long way home,
    the careful steps,
    the gradual reentry,
    the grace that makes space
    for healing to become wholeness.

Until every exile finds their way back,
    until every stigma is lifted,
    until the living bird of freedom flies
    over all who've been bound,
    keep us walking the path of restoration.

Blessed are you, God who brings the outcast home.
Blessed are you, Christ who meets us outside the camp.
Blessed are you, Spirit who anoints us for new life.

Amen.

Bodies Before God (Leviticus 15)

God who made us flesh and blood,
      you don't turn away from our bodies
      in all their awkward, leaking, mortal reality.
You speak of what we whisper about,
      name what we try to hide,
      and make room in your law
      for the rhythms of our physical lives.
You remind us that we're dust,
      that life flows through us and from us,
      and that even our bodies must be brought before you
      in honesty and reverence.

We confess our shame about our bodies.
We treat our flesh as something less than holy,
      hide what's natural,
      despise what's human.
We've made the body a source of disgust
      rather than a dwelling place of your Spirit.
We've let silence and stigma
      replace honest conversation about our physical selves.
We've forgotten that you dwell among us
      even in our uncleanness.

We lament the shame heaped upon bodies
      for doing what bodies do.
We grieve for those whose cycles and conditions

have been treated as curse rather than creation,
who've been excluded and isolated
for what they could not control.
We mourn the silence around illness,
    the stigma around disease,
    the loneliness of those whose bodies betray them
    and find no welcome in community.

Yet you, O Lord, became flesh yourself.
You entered the mess and mystery of embodiment,
    sweating, bleeding, weeping, dying.
When a woman with a flow of blood touched your garment,
    you didn't recoil,
    you turned, you saw, you healed.
You reversed the flow of uncleanness:
    your touch makes clean what was defiled.
Even now, you sanctify our mortal frames
    and call us to live without shame.

So free us, Lord, from the prison of shame.
Teach us to honor our bodies as you do,
    to speak with wisdom about what's natural,
    to care for our flesh without contempt.
Heal those who suffer in silence,
    whose conditions isolate them,
    whose bodies carry burdens unseen.
Even now, remind us that you dwell among us,
    tabernacle with us,
    even in our frailty.

Make us a people who honor the body
    as temple and gift,
    who speak honestly about health and illness,

who create communities where no one hides in shame.
Help us see that every washing,
     every waiting until evening,
     every return to community
     is a small picture of your renewing grace.

Until our bodies are raised imperishable,
     until every weakness is transformed to strength,
     until mortality puts on immortality,
     keep us living as embodied souls
     who carry your presence in vessels of clay.

Blessed are you, God who formed us from dust.
Blessed are you, Christ who took on flesh for our sake.
Blessed are you, Spirit who dwells in these mortal bodies.

Amen.

The Day All Is Made Right (Leviticus 16)

God of mercy and atonement,
      you gave your people a day
      when every sin could be confessed,
      every uncleanness addressed,
      every broken thing brought into your holy presence
      and made right.
You alone could enter the Most Holy Place,
      hidden in clouds of incense,
      sprinkling blood upon the mercy seat,
      carrying the weight of a people's transgression
      into the presence of unapproachable glory.
You designed a day when the slate is wiped clean.

We confess that we carry sins
      we've not named,
      guilt we've not acknowledged,
      transgressions we've hidden even from ourselves.
We live as if atonement were unnecessary,
      as if we could manage our own reconciliation,
      as if the distance between your holiness and our sin
      weren't the chasm it truly is.
We've grown casual with grace
      and forgotten the cost of cleansing.

We lament the weight of accumulated sin:
      personal failures that compound,

communal wrongs that stain generations,
systemic evils that defile the land.
We grieve the harm we've done
knowingly and unknowingly,
the relationships fractured,
the trust betrayed,
the holiness defiled.
We mourn a world desperately in need
of a day when all is made right.

Yet you, O Lord, have provided the Way.
One goat was slain, blood sprinkled seven times,
atonement made for sanctuary and people.
Another goat bore the sins of all,
sent into the wilderness,
carrying transgression far from the camp,
never to return.
And in the fullness of time,
your Son became both sacrifice and scapegoat:
blood shed to cover,
sins carried away forever.
Even now, the veil is torn,
and we may enter boldly
into the presence once forbidden.

So cleanse us, God of atonement.
Sprinkle us with the blood that purifies.
Lay your hands upon the scapegoat of our souls
and send our sins into the wilderness,
to a land uninhabited,
never to be found again.
Cleanse what has been defiled:
our hearts, our homes, our communities.

Even now, let this be a day of rest and renewal,
     when we afflict our souls
     and find ourselves made clean.

Make us a people who live in the freedom of atonement,
     who confess without hiding,
     who receive forgiveness without grasping for merit,
     who extend to others the grace we've received.
Help us live as those whose sins have been removed
     as far as the east is from the west,
     as far as the wilderness stretches
     beyond the reach of memory.

Until the final Day of Atonement,
     when every wrong is made right,
     when the blood of the Lamb covers all creation,
     when we stand before the mercy seat
     with nothing to hide,
     keep us living in the power of your cleansing.

Blessed are you, God who atones for our sin.
Blessed are you, Christ our sacrifice and scapegoat.
Blessed are you, Spirit who applies the blood that cleanses.

Amen.

The Life Is in the Blood (Leviticus 17)

God of life and God of atonement,
> you've taught us that the life of every creature
> is in the blood,
> and you've given it to us upon the altar
> to make atonement for our souls.
Blood isn't common to you;
> it's sacred, costly, the currency of redemption.
You're the giver of life,
> the one who breathed into dust and made it living,
> and every pulse of blood
> is a gift from your hand.

We confess how cheaply we hold life.
We spill blood without thought,
> consume without gratitude,
> take what was given without acknowledging the Giver.
We treat the death of creatures as meaningless
> and forget that every life laid down
> points toward the one Life
> that would be given for all.
We've grown casual with sacrifice,
> numb to the cost of atonement,
> blind to the blood that covers us.

We lament the blood unjustly shed:
> the violence that stains our streets,

the wars that drain nations of their young,
        the exploitation that treats lives as expendable.
We grieve the blood that cries out from the ground,
        the innocent slain,
        the vulnerable crushed,
        the voiceless silenced.
We mourn a world that has forgotten
        the sacredness of what pulses through every vein.

Yet you, O Lord, haven't forgotten.
You gave the blood of bulls and goats
        as a shadow of good things to come,
        a dim preview of the perfect sacrifice.
And in the fullness of time,
        you gave what no animal could give:
        your own blood,
        the life of the Son poured out,
        not to cover sin for a season
        but to take it away forever.
The blood that makes atonement
        has been shed once for all.
Even now, we're cleansed, forgiven,
        made right by the blood of the Lamb.

So teach us, Lord, to reverence life.
Help us see the sacredness in every creature,
        the gift in every breath,
        the cost in every drop of blood.
Keep us from growing numb
        to the sacrifice that saved us.
Let the blood of Christ
        never become ordinary to our hearts.
Even now, apply to us

the atonement you've provided,
and make us people who honor life
because we know its cost.

Make us a people who protect the vulnerable,
    who refuse to shed blood unjustly,
    who honor the life in every creature
    as a gift from your hand.
Help us live as those who have been bought
    with a price beyond measure,
    who carry in our veins
    the memory of the blood that saved us.

Until the day when no blood is shed in violence,
    until death itself is swallowed up,
    until the life that was given
    fills all things with resurrection glory,
    keep us living in the power of the blood
    that speaks a better word than Abel's.

Blessed are you, God who gives life.
Blessed are you, Christ whose blood atones.
Blessed are you, Spirit who applies the sacrifice
    and makes us alive forevermore.

Amen.

Boundaries That Bless (Leviticus 18)

God who calls us to be different,
>you've set your people apart
>from the practices of Egypt and Canaan,
>from customs that corrupt and destroy.

You're the Lord our God,
>and in your laws we find life.

Your boundaries aren't arbitrary;
>they're wisdom shaped into commands,
>protection woven into prohibition,
>love expressed as limitation.

You guard the vulnerable,
>honor the bonds of family,
>and call us to a holiness
>that reflects your own character.

We confess how often we've crossed your boundaries.

We've followed the customs of cultures
>that treat bodies as objects,
>intimacy as entertainment,
>and desire as its own justification.

We've dishonored parents,
>betrayed spouses,
>exploited the vulnerable,
>and called it freedom.

We've consumed images that defile,
>fed fantasies that corrupt,

and wandered far from the wholeness you intend.
Forgive us, Lord,
and restore to us the beauty of your design.

We lament the devastation
when your boundaries are ignored.
We grieve for children harmed by those who should protect them,
for families torn apart by betrayal,
for the vulnerable exploited by the powerful.
We mourn the epidemic of abuse,
the trafficking of bodies,
the addiction to images that destroy.
We weep for those who carry wounds
inflicted by those who crossed lines
that should never have been crossed.
We cry out for a world
that has forgotten how to protect the sacred.

Yet you, O Lord, are a God who restores.
You don't leave us in our defilement
but offer cleansing, healing, new beginning.
Your grace meets us in our brokenness
and calls us back to wholeness.
Jesus touched the untouchable,
welcomed the ashamed,
and offered living water
to those who had searched for love
in all the wrong places.
Even now, you're making all things new,
teaching us that your commands
aren't burdens but blessings,
pathways to the abundant life
you always intended for your children.

So guard our hearts, O God.
Teach us to honor your boundaries
        as expressions of your love.
Protect the vulnerable among us:
        children, spouses, the exploited.
Give us strength to resist
        the customs of cultures that defile.
Heal those who have been harmed
        by the crossing of sacred lines.
Even now, renew our minds,
        purify our desires,
        and set our feet on the path of life.

Make us a people who protect the sacred,
        who honor bodies as temples,
        who treat intimacy as holy gift.
Help us build families where trust is honored,
        communities where the vulnerable are safe,
        and churches where grace and truth walk together.
We won't follow the practices
        of Egypt or Canaan or the cultures around us.
We'll walk in your statutes
        and find life through them.

Until the day when all exploitation ceases,
        until every wound is healed,
        until your design for human flourishing
        is fully realized in your kingdom,
        keep us walking in the boundaries
        that lead to life.

Blessed are you, God who sets us apart.

Blessed are you, Christ who cleanses and restores.
Blessed are you, Spirit who empowers holy living.

Amen.

Be Holy, For I Am Holy (Leviticus 19)

Holy God, who calls us to be holy
    as you're holy,
    you've shown us that holiness isn't abstraction
    but a way of living with one another.
You're the God who commands us
    to leave the corners of our fields for
        those experiencing poverty,
    to pay wages before the sun sets,
    to refuse the stumbling block before the blind
    and the curse against the deaf.
You're the God who thunders:
    "Love your neighbor as yourself."
Fifteen times in this single chapter
    you declare: "I'm the Lord"
    as if to say: this is who I am,
    and this is who you must become.

We confess how far we fall
    from this holiness that loves.
We've harvested every corner for ourselves,
    leaving nothing for those experiencing poverty to glean.
We've delayed the wages of those who work for us,
    exploiting their need for our gain.
We've cursed those who can't hear our contempt
    and laid stumbling blocks before those who can't see.
We've spread slander among our people,

nursed grudges in our hearts,
    and sought revenge rather than reconciliation.
We've used dishonest scales in our dealings,
    twisted justice to favor the powerful,
    and mistreated the stranger in our land.
Forgive us, Lord.
We've claimed holiness
    while ignoring our neighbors.

We lament a world that's forgotten
    how to be neighbor to one another.
We grieve for those experiencing poverty who glean nothing
    because we've harvested every grain.
We weep for workers whose wages are stolen,
    whose labor is exploited,
    whose dignity is denied.
We mourn for the disabled mocked and excluded,
    for the elderly forgotten and dismissed,
    for the stranger mistreated and feared.
We cry out against systems rigged with dishonest scales,
    courts corrupted by partiality,
    communities poisoned by slander and grudge.
How long, O Lord,
    until we learn to love?

Yet you, O God, haven't abandoned us
    to our failures of love.
You sent your Son to fulfill this law,
    to embody perfect neighbor-love.
Jesus touched the leper others wouldn't touch,
    spoke to the woman others wouldn't see,
    welcomed the outcast others had excluded.
He opened eyes of the blind,

unstopped ears of the deaf,
and proclaimed good news to those experiencing poverty.
When asked "Who's my neighbor?"
he told of a Samaritan, a stranger
who stopped to bind wounds
when the righteous passed by.
Even now, through his Spirit,
He's teaching us to love as he loved,
to be holy as he's holy.

So teach us, Lord, this holiness that loves.
Give us generous hands
that leave corners for those experiencing poverty to glean.
Give us honest scales
that deal fairly with all.
Give us reverence for the elderly
and welcome for the stranger.
Give us tongues that refuse slander
and hearts that release grudges.
Help us see in every person,
poor or powerful, native or stranger,
able-bodied or disabled,
a neighbor to be loved as ourselves.
Even now, form in us
the character of your Son,
who loved his neighbor unto death.

Make us a people of holy love.
We'll leave margins of generosity
for those who have less than we do.
We'll pay fair wages promptly
and refuse to exploit the vulnerable.
We'll rise in the presence of the elderly

and treat the stranger as one born among us.
We'll judge with impartiality,
    speak with honesty,
    and deal with integrity.
We'll rebuke when necessary
    but never nurse hatred in our hearts.
We'll love our neighbors as ourselves,
    remembering that we were once strangers
    and you loved us.

Until the day when every neighbor is loved,
    until those experiencing poverty glean abundantly
    from the generous margins of your kingdom,
    until the stranger is stranger no more
    but welcomed as family,
    until justice rolls down like waters
    and righteousness like an ever-flowing stream,
    keep us walking in the way of love
    that is the way of holiness.

Blessed are you, Holy God,
    who calls us to be like yourself.
Blessed are you, Christ who loved your neighbor
    even to the point of death.
Blessed are you, Spirit who pours out love
    into our hearts and makes us holy.
You're the Lord.

Amen.

The Weight of What We Do (Leviticus 20)

God of justice,
>> you don't look away from evil
>> or pretend that sin has no consequence.
You set your face against those who sacrifice children to Molech,
>> who pursue dark powers instead of you.
You take sin seriously
>> because you love what sin destroys.
You're the Lord who sanctifies
>> the one who makes us holy.

We confess that we've minimized sin,
>> calling evil a "mistake" and harm a "poor choice."
We've hidden our eyes from atrocities we didn't want to see
>> and become accessories by our silence.
We've sacrificed our children to the Molechs of our age
>> to ambition, addiction,
>> and ideologies that devour the young.
We've sought guidance from dark places
>> instead of turning to you alone.
Forgive us, Lord.
We've forgotten that sin is serious
>> because life is sacred.

We lament the devastation sin has wrought:
>> children sacrificed on altars of greed and power,
>> families shattered by betrayal,

those trapped in cycles they can't break.
We cry out for a world
        that has lost the language of sin and judgment,
        and so can't find the path to repentance and life.

Yet your judgment isn't cruelty;
        it's the measure of how much you care.
And you didn't leave us under its weight alone.
You sent your Son to bear the penalty we deserved,
        to become a curse for us
        so we might receive blessing.
The one who knew no sin became sin for us,
        so that in him
        we might become the righteousness of God.
You're the Lord who sanctifies
        and even now, you're making us holy.

Give us holy fear.
Help us see sin as you see it.
Give us courage to name evil
        and protect the vulnerable from harm.
Guard us from every idol
        that demands we sacrifice what's most precious.
Even now, sanctify us
        by the blood of Christ and the power of your Spirit.

Make us a people who take sin seriously
        because we take grace seriously.
We won't hide our eyes from evil.
We'll protect children from every Molech.
We'll be holy,
        for you, the Lord our God, are holy.

Until the day when every wrong is righted,
        until justice and mercy meet,
        until sin is no more,
        keep us walking in the light,
        clinging to the grace that saves.

Blessed are you, God of justice,
        who doesn't ignore our sin.
Blessed are you, Christ who bore our judgment.
Blessed are you, Spirit who sanctifies,
making us holy as God is holy.

Amen.

A Priest Without Defect (Leviticus 21)

God who dwells in unapproachable light,
> you set apart priests to stand before you,
> to offer the bread of your presence,
> to bridge the gap between holy and common.

You required of them a higher standard:
> no contact with death,
> no compromising marriages,
> no defects that would disqualify their service.

The threefold holiness you established,
> people, priests, high priest,
> mirrored the threefold sanctuary:
> outer court, holy place, most holy.

You're the Lord who sanctifies,
> and you require those who draw near
> to reflect your perfection.

We confess that we approach you carelessly.
We forget that your presence demands reverence,
> that drawing near is costly.

We've offered you our leftovers,
> our distracted worship,
> our compromised lives.

We haven't examined ourselves
> before coming to your table.

Forgive us, Lord.
We're defective priests serving a perfect God.

We lament the gap
>between your holiness and our brokenness.
None of us is without defect,
>none qualified to approach on our own merit.
We grieve for those told they were too broken for your service,
>too flawed for your presence.
We weep for those wounded by failed mediators
>leaders whose hidden defects
>hurt those in their care.

Yet in this very requirement we find our hope.
You knew we could never produce a priest without defect,
>and so you provided one yourself:
Jesus Christ, our great High Priest
>holy, blameless, pure,
>set apart from sinners,
>exalted above the heavens.
He entered heaven itself with his own blood,
>lives forever to intercede,
>and through him we have access to the throne of grace.
The veil is torn.
The way is open.
Even the broken may draw near.

Clothe us in the righteousness of Christ.
We can't make ourselves worthy,
>but he has made us worthy.
Help those told they're too broken
>to know that Christ qualifies them.
Heal those wounded by failed mediators,
>and show them the one Mediator who'll never fail.
Draw us into your presence

through the blood of Jesus.

Make us a royal priesthood, a holy nation.
Though defective in ourselves,
        in Christ we're clothed with his perfection.
We'll approach with confidence
        not because of our worthiness but because of his.
We'll live as priests,
        bringing others into your presence
        and declaring your praises.

Until the day when every defect is healed,
        until we see you face to face,
        keep us drawing near with confidence
        to the throne of grace.

Blessed are you, Holy God,
        who dwells in unapproachable light.
Blessed are you, Christ our High Priest,
        holy, blameless, undefiled.
Blessed are you, Spirit
        who makes us a kingdom of priests to our God.

Amen.

Without Blemish (Leviticus 22)

God who deserves our best,
>> you commanded that offerings be without defect,
>> without blemish, without flaw.
Not the blind, the injured, the maimed;
>> not the cast-offs we wouldn't miss.
You asked for the best of the flock
>> because you're worthy of the best we have.
To bring a defective gift to you
>> wouldn't be worship but insult.
You're the Lord who makes us holy,
>> and you won't be profaned.

We confess how often we offer you our leftovers:
>> the scraps of our time,
>> the margins of our attention,
>> the parts of our lives we weren't using anyway.
We give you what costs us nothing
>> and call it devotion.
We approach your presence carelessly,
>> treating sacred things with contempt.
Forgive us, Lord.
We have offered the blemished
>> when you deserve the whole.

We lament worship that has become routine,
>> offerings given without thought,

service rendered without heart.
We grieve for a world that reserves its best
    for lesser things,
    for careers, comforts, pleasures,
    and gives you the remainder.

Yet you, O God, did not offer us your leftovers.
You gave your best:
    your only Son,
    the Lamb without blemish or defect.
He wasn't blind, injured, or maimed,
    but perfect in every way,
    and still you gave him for us.
The one offering that would be accepted on our behalf
    was offered once for all.
In him, we who are blemished
    are made acceptable to you.

Teach us to offer you our best.
Not because you need it,
    but because you deserve it.
Receive the offering of our lives,
    imperfect as they are,
    and make them acceptable through Christ.
Even now, cleanse us
    so we may handle holy things with reverence.

We won't offer you what costs us nothing.
We'll bring our firstfruits, not our leftovers;
    our best hours, not our spare moments;
    our whole hearts, not our divided attention.
We'll treat your holy name with reverence,
    for you're the Lord who makes us holy.

Until the day when every offering is pure,
    until all worship rises without blemish,
    keep us bringing you our best,
    made acceptable through the perfect Lamb.

Blessed are you, God who deserves our all.
Blessed are you, Christ the unblemished offering.
Blessed are you, Spirit who makes our worship acceptable.

Amen.

The Rhythm of Sacred Time (Leviticus 23)

God who orders time itself,
>> you gave your people appointed feasts:
>> Sabbath rest each seventh day,
>> Passover to remember deliverance,
>> Firstfruits to honor the harvest's beginning,
>> Pentecost to celebrate the ingathering,
>> Trumpets to announce the sacred season,
>> Atonement to cleanse the nation's sin,
>> Tabernacles to dwell in holy remembrance.

You wove worship into the calendar,
>> made sacred assemblies the rhythm of life,
>> and called your people to stop, remember, and rejoice.

We confess that we have lost the rhythm.
We fill our calendars with everything but you.
We work without ceasing,
>> ignore the Sabbath you commanded,
>> and wonder why our souls are exhausted.

We rarely stop to remember your deliverance
>> or gather in sacred assembly.

Forgive us, Lord.
We have made time for everything but worship.

We lament a world without sabbath,
>> without feast days that interrupt our striving,
>> without rhythms that remind us who we are.

We grieve the burnout, the exhaustion,
    the relentless pace that leaves no room for God.
We mourn communities that no longer gather
    to remember, repent, and rejoice together.

Yet every feast pointed forward to Christ.
He is our Passover Lamb, slain for our deliverance.
He is the Firstfruits, risen from the dead.
At Pentecost, his Spirit was poured out.
He is our Atonement, making us right with God.
He tabernacled among us, full of grace and truth.
The feasts find their fulfillment in him,
    and still he invites us into sacred rhythm:
    rest, remembrance, and rejoicing.

Restore to us the gift of holy time.
Teach us again to keep Sabbath,
    to gather in sacred assembly,
    to let the rhythm of worship order our days.
Even now, interrupt our striving with your rest.

We'll honor the rhythms you have given.
We'll stop to remember your deliverance,
    gather with your people in holy assembly,
    and let our calendars reflect your lordship.
We won't let work crowd out worship
    or hurry silence the invitation to rest.

Until the final feast is celebrated,
    until we dwell with you in eternal tabernacles,
    keep us in the rhythm of grace:
    resting, remembering, rejoicing in you.

Blessed are you, God who hallows time.

Blessed are you, Christ in whom every feast finds meaning.

Blessed are you, Spirit who gathers us still.

Amen.

Light and Bread and Holy Name (Leviticus 24)

God whose lamp burns continually,
>you commanded pure oil for the lampstand,
>tended from evening to morning,
>light that never went out in your dwelling.

You ordered twelve loaves set before you,
>bread of presence, renewed each Sabbath,
>a sign of your provision for every tribe.

And you guarded your name as holy
>not to be cursed, not to be profaned,
>for in your name is your very nature.

We confess that we've let the light grow dim.
We've neglected the daily tending,
>the morning and evening attention
>that keeps faith burning bright.

We've taken your provision for granted,
>eating without gratitude,
>receiving without remembering the Giver.

We've used your name carelessly
>in casual oaths, in empty worship,
>in lives that contradict what we profess.

Forgive us, Lord.

We lament the darkness that spreads
>when your light is neglected.

We grieve a world where your name is blasphemed,

mocked, weaponized, made meaningless.
We mourn our own hypocrisy
    claiming your name while dishonoring it
    by how we live.

Yet you didn't leave us in darkness.
Christ declared: I'm the light of the world.
Whoever follows me won't walk in darkness
    but will have the light of life.
He said: I'm the bread of life.
Whoever comes to me will never hunger.
The lampstand pointed to him;
    the showbread was his shadow.
And though he was falsely accused of blasphemy,
    he bore our curse and hallowed your name.

Teach us to tend the light daily,
    morning and evening seeking your face.
Feed us with the bread of your presence.
Make your name holy on our lips
    spoken with reverence, lived with integrity.

We'll keep the lamp burning.
We'll come to the table you have set.
We'll hallow your name
    in word and deed and thought.
We'll shine as lights in the world,
    reflecting the one true Light.

Until the city that needs no sun,
    for the Lamb is its lamp;
    until we eat at your table forever,
    keep us in your light.

Blessed are you, God whose presence never dims.
Blessed are you, Christ our light and our bread.
Blessed are you, Spirit who makes your name holy in us.

Amen.

Proclaim Liberty (Leviticus 25)

God who gives rest to land and people,
>   you commanded a Sabbath for the soil
>   six years to sow, one year to lie fallow,
>   trusting you to provide from what grows wild.
And every fiftieth year, you ordained Jubilee:
>   trumpet blast on the Day of Atonement,
>   liberty proclaimed throughout the land,
>   slaves set free, debts forgiven,
>   every family returned to their inheritance.
The land is yours, you said;
>   we're strangers and sojourners with you.

We confess that we resist your rest.
We exploit without ceasing,
>   extract without replenishing,
>   accumulate without releasing.
We act as if we own what's only entrusted.
We cling to what should circulate,
>   hoard what should be shared,
>   and call permanent what you meant to be temporary.
Forgive us, Lord.
We have forgotten we are guests in your world.

We lament the exhaustion of land and people,
>   economies that know no Sabbath,
>   systems where debts compound for generations

and those experiencing poverty never find release.
We grieve families separated by poverty,
> inheritances lost and never restored,
> the powerful ruling ruthlessly over the weak.

Yet you sent one to proclaim Jubilee fulfilled.
In Nazareth's synagogue, Jesus read:
The Spirit of the Lord is upon me
> to proclaim good news to the poor,
> liberty to the captives,
> the year of the Lord's favor.
Today, he said, this is fulfilled.
> He's our kinsman-redeemer,
> buying back what we had sold,
> restoring us to our true inheritance.

Teach us to live as Jubilee people.
Give us courage to rest and let rest,
> to release and restore,
> to forgive debts as we've been forgiven.
Make us agents of liberty in a world still captive.

We'll hold loosely what's not ours to keep.
We'll remember that we're stewards, not owners.
We'll practice release and restoration,
> living toward the Jubilee that is coming.

Until the final trumpet sounds,
> until every captive is free,
> until we enter our eternal inheritance,
> keep us faithful to your economy of grace.

Blessed are you, God who owns all things.
Blessed are you, Christ our Jubilee.
Blessed are you, Spirit of liberty.

Amen.

I Will Walk Among You (Leviticus 26)

God who keeps covenant,
>   you promised blessing for obedience:
>   rain in its season, harvest in abundance,
>   peace in the land, victory over enemies,
>   and this, the greatest blessing of all
>   I'll walk among you
>   and be your God,
>   and you'll be my people.

You also warned of curse for disobedience:
>   terror and disease, defeat and exile,
>   discipline escalating until hearts would turn.

Even your judgment aimed at restoration.

We confess that we've walked contrary to you.
We've despised your statutes,
>   abhorred your ordinances,
>   broken the covenant you made with us.
>   Our hearts have been uncircumcised
>   hard, resistant, proud.

We confess our iniquity
>   and the iniquity of our fathers.

We accept the punishment of our guilt.
Have mercy, Lord.

We lament the harvest of our rebellion:
>   broken families, scattered communities,

the desolation that follows disobedience.
We grieve a world that's forgotten its God
and reaps what it's sown.

Yet even in exile, you promised:
I won't cast them away,
I won't abhor them to destroy them utterly,
I won't break my covenant.
For I'm the Lord their God.
And now in Christ, all the curses we deserved
fell upon him who hung on a tree.
He became a curse for us
so that the blessing might come to us.
All the promises find their Yes in him.

Circumcise our hearts.
Humble our proud spirits.
Remember your covenant
not because we deserve it,
but because you're faithful.
Walk among us still.

We won't make idols or bow to images.
We'll keep your Sabbaths
and reverence your sanctuary.
We'll walk in your statutes,
not to earn your blessing
but because we've already received it in Christ.

Until you dwell with us forever,
until every tear is wiped away,
until curse gives way to blessing eternal
keep us faithful to the covenant sealed in blood.

Blessed are you, God who remembers your covenant.
Blessed are you, Christ who bore our curse.
Blessed are you, Spirit who writes the law on our hearts.

Amen.

Vows and Valuations (Leviticus 27)

God who weighs all things,
      you taught your people to take vows seriously:
      persons dedicated, animals consecrated,
      houses and fields set apart for your service.
You set the price of redemption
      and made provision for those experiencing poverty.
What passes our lips matters.
A vow spoken is a vow that must be kept.

We confess that we've made vows lightly
      and broken promises easily.
We've dedicated ourselves in moments of desperation
      then forgotten when the crisis passed.
We've withheld the tithe that belongs to you,
      kept back what was already yours.
We've substituted the inferior for the best,
      hoping you wouldn't notice.
Forgive our careless words and casual commitments.

We grieve a world where promises mean little,
      where vows are made to be broken,
      where words have lost their weight.
We lament our own divided hearts
      that long to give you everything
      yet keep crawling off the altar.

Yet you've made a vow you will never break.
You promised Abraham blessing,
        promised Eve a seed to crush the serpent's head.
And you paid the price of your own vow
        in the blood of your Son.
He's the redemption we could never afford,
        the valuation beyond all silver and gold.
We were bought with a price
        and now belong to you.

Teach us to let our yes be yes
        and our no be no.
Make us people of our word
        because we serve the God who keeps his.
Help us honor commitments made in your name.

We present our bodies as living sacrifices,
        holy and acceptable to you.
We dedicate ourselves afresh this day:
        our time, our resources, our very selves.
We won't substitute the lesser for the greater
        or hold back what already belongs to you.
The earth is yours and everything in it.
We're stewards, never owners.

Until the day we see you face to face,
        until every vow finds its fulfillment,
        until we worship in the temple not made with hands,
        keep us faithful to what we've promised.

Blessed are you, God who keeps every promise.

Blessed are you, Christ who paid our redemption.

Blessed are you, Spirit who seals us as God's own.

Amen.

The Holy Fire Among Us: A Prayer for the Whole of Leviticus

God of holiness and nearness,
　　　　you've called us into the center of your dwelling,
　　　　into courts fragrant with offering,
　　　　into rhythms of rest and remembrance.
You've taught us how to draw near without fear,
　　　　how to live with fire in our midst,
　　　　and how to let your presence shape the pattern of our lives.

We give you thanks for every cleansing,
　　　　the ones we felt like cool water on parched hearts,
　　　　and the ones that healed us in ways unseen.
You've lifted burdens we couldn't name,
　　　　restored what shame had stolen,
　　　　and clothed us in the dignity of those beloved by God.

Even now, you make sacred the ordinary.
　　　　Even now, you breathe holiness into our habits,
　　　　turn work into worship,
　　　　fill silence with your welcome.
You dwell not only in sanctuaries of stone,
　　　　but in every act of justice,
　　　　every moment of mercy,
　　　　every community formed by your love.

We confess that holiness intimidates us.
We prefer the comfort of compromise
		to the courage of consecration.
But you, O Lord, keep inviting,
		teaching us that holiness isn't distance,
		but deep belonging;
		not severity,
		but the slow beauty of becoming whole.

So, send us forth, O God of Leviticus,
		with hearts purified by your compassion
		and lives ordered by your wisdom.
Make our communities tabernacles of welcome,
		our homes places of rest,
		our work a fragrant offering of love.

Until every life bears the imprint of your presence,
		until all creation is healed by your mercy,
		until the world shines with the beauty of holiness,
		keep us living in the light of your fire.

Blessed are you, God who dwells and sanctifies,
		whose holiness is love made visible.
Blessed are you, Christ our atonement and peace,
		whose life draws us near.
Blessed are you, Spirit of consecration,
		whose fire burns gently within us.

Amen.

Benediction: To Those Who Carry the Holy Fire

Go now, children of presence and promise.
Walk in the rhythm shaped by sacrifice and song.
Carry the fragrance of prayers that rose like incense,
    and the memory of mercy that made you clean.
Let your steps keep the cadence of holiness,
    not the harshness of perfection,
    but the tenderness of belonging.

Remember the God who draws near,
    who dwells not beyond the veil
    but in the beating of your own faithful heart.
The One who teaches you to rest,
    who anoints your work with meaning,
    who binds justice and compassion into a single, radiant life.

Let your days become a sanctuary of welcome,
    your words a blessing offered freely,
    your hands a witness to the God who consecrates the ordinary.
Let your presence carry peace
    like priests who bear the names of the beloved
    over their hearts.

And when holiness feels heavy
    or the path feels too narrow,
    remember: the Fire that calls you
    is also the Fire that keeps you.

The Presence walks beside you
>> in desert heat and Sabbath quiet,
>> and the Mercy that once met you at the altar
>> still meets you in the hidden hours.

The journey isn't finished;
>> the invitation hasn't faded.
The Holy One still speaks your name,
>> still fills your life with glory,
>> still makes you a dwelling place of grace.

Go in peace, beloved of God,
>> and carry the holy fire into the world.

Amen.

Appendix 1: Would You Help?

Writing a book takes immense effort. It's a sustained labor of love over months, even years. Every page carries hours of thought, prayer, revision, and hope. And while the writing may be solitary, the life of a book is communal. That's where you come in. If this book has meant something to you, I'd be deeply grateful if you could help it find its way into more hands and hearts.

There are two simple but powerful ways you can do that.

First, consider leaving a short review on Amazon (and Goodreads would be wonderful too). Even just a few sentences can help others discover the book, as reviews significantly influence how books are recommended and shared online. You can do that by visiting Amazon or searching for this book and writing a review. Even a short note helps people find the book.

Second, if the book has stirred something in you, would you share it with others: friends, groups, churches, or anyone who might benefit from its message?

Your support helps keep this work going, and it means more than I can say. Thank you for being part of this journey.

Find this book on these pages:
1. Amazon:
https://www.amazon.com.au/stores/author/B008NI4ORQ
2. Goodreads:
https://www.goodreads.com/author/show/20347171.Graham_Joseph _Hill

3. Author Website:

https://grahamjosephhill.com/books/

Appendix 2: About Me

Graham Joseph Hill (OAM, PhD) is an Adjunct Research Fellow and Associate Professor at Charles Sturt University, and one of Australia's most prolific and awarded Christian authors. He's written more than thirty books, including *Salt, Light, and a City*, which was named Jesus Creed's 2012 Book of the Year (church category); *Healing Our Broken Humanity* (with Grace Ji-Sun Kim), named Outreach Magazine's 2019 Resource of the Year (culture category); and *World Christianity*, shortlisted for the 2025 Australian Christian Book of the Year. In 2024, Graham was awarded the Medal of the Order of Australia (OAM) for his service to theological education. He lives in Sydney with his wife, Shyn.

Author and Ministry Websites

GrahamJosephHill.com

GrahamJosephHill.Substack.com

youtube.com/@GrahamJosephHill_Author

Linktr.ee/dailydevotions

facebook.com/grahamjosephhill/

instagram.com/grahamjosephhill/

amazon.com.au/stores/author/B008NI4ORQ

goodreads.com/author/show/20347171.Graham_Joseph_Hill

Books

See all my books at GrahamJosephHill.com/books

Appendix 3: Connect With Me

I'd love to stay connected with you. You can sign up to my Substack, Spirituality and Society with Hilly, where I share new writing, spiritual reflections, and updates on future books. Please find me on Substack: https://grahamjosephhill.substack.com

You can also find my books on my website:
https://grahamjosephhill.com/books

You can also connect with me through my Facebook author page:
https://www.facebook.com/GrahamJosephHill/